Virtual Assistant Training, A Complete Guide Work From Home

SADANAND PUJARI

Published by SADANAND PUJARI, 2023.

Table of Contents

Copyright 1

About 2

Chapter 1 4

Chapter 2 6

Chapter 3 7

Chapter 4 9

Chapter 5 10

Chapter 6 11

Chapter 7 12

Chapter 8 13

Chapter 9 14

Chapter 10 15

Chapter 11 16

Chapter 12 17

Chapter 13 18

Chapter 14 19

Chapter 15 20

Chapter 16 21

Chapter 17 22

Chapter 18 23

Chapter 19 24

Chapter 20 25

Chapter 21 26

Chapter 22 29

Chapter 23 32

Chapter 24 33

Chapter 25 34

Chapter 26 35

Chapter 27 36

Chapter 28 37

Chapter 29 38

Chapter 30 40

Chapter 31 42

Chapter 32 48

Important Interview Questions 54

Chapter 34 55

Chapter 35 61

Chapter 36..65

Conclusion...66

Copyright

Copyright © 2023 by **SADANAND PUJARI**

All rights reserved. No part of this book may be reproduced, scanned, or distributed in any printed or electronic form without permission. Please do not participate in or encourage piracy of copyrighted materials in violation of the author's rights. Purchase only authorized editions.

Virtual Assistant Training, A Complete Guide Work From Home

First Edition: Dec 2023

Book Design by **SADANAND PUJARI**

About

Live life on your terms as a Virtual Assistant. Do you want to make a living while being in the comfort of your own home? Do you want to create multiple streams of income?

Do you want to land a high paying and quality virtual assistant position but not sure where to start? Have you ever dreamed of being your own boss or being able to work from anywhere in the world? Being a virtual assistant or virtual worker means earning money on your own terms.

Working virtually or remotely gives you more freedom and control over your schedule, plus more free time as you no longer have to commute! You're also not limited only to positions that are close to home, as you can work for companies anywhere in the world. Depending on your skill set, you can earn more without having to move for a new position or increasing your work hours.

The virtual assistance and freelance business today is not only huge, but immensely thriving. You may have the skillset, tools and knowledge, but if you don't know when, where, and how to market yourself as a virtual assistant, your options are limited.

In this Book, you will learn how to start your Virtual Assistance business tailored and customized for YOU, depending on what your ideal client or employer is and what your niche or specialty is.

In this virtual assistant training you will learn how to find the right clients and get hired, how to avoid scams, and how to set your price. In this virtual assistant training I will also provide a series of knowledgebase for every Virtual Assistant Skill you need to master to be a successful virtual assistant.

Virtual Assistant Training Complete Guide is suitable for both beginner to advanced VA's, as here we discuss the principles and foundations of being a virtual assistant, as well as continuing to develop your virtual assistant career.

Chapter 1

Hi, welcome to Taking the Leap and joining the Kukes. In this chapter, I would like to give you some information about me. You would then have the opportunity to introduce yourself to the Book community to give you a very quick rundown of my career. I started my career at the age of 11. I was the kid that started in school by the age of 14.

I had seven mobile games published on Plaistow , of which two were sold. And now the collection consists of 18 mobile games by the age of 17. I opened my first restaurant which I sold at 19 in 2020. I launched my first book called The Persuasive Marketer, which reached number one bestseller on Amazon and is currently the CEO and founder, a group that consists of multiple companies that create outside the box solutions to common corporate issues in terms of medication background.

I have to distension store and national extended diploma in information technology and a first class honors degree in information technology management for business. Now that you know about me, I want to know more about you. Please introduce yourself to the community using the features of the platform. Let's build each other up. If you have any questions concerning this Book, please feel free to message me using the built in messaging feature of the platform, and I will try to get back to you within 24 hours.

Once again, I want to say thank you for joining, and I'm sure you will have a fantastic learning experience in this Book. Besides that, I look forward to seeing you guys in the Book community and learning more about it.

Chapter 2

Great question you may be having is how do you use this Book? What are you going to get from it and why is this Book is just like my other ones? We would be doing the theory of what first alerted the essential bits first. And then if I see fit the Book, I will do the practical and show you exactly how you do it step by step.

So you can do the same after all of this introduction, stuff of me explaining the basics where went straight into it and will literally start from step one all the way to the end by the end of the Book, would be experienced in the topic and allowing you to make informative decisions in the same day you are taking the Book is not going to be an overly long Book.

It's just going to be precise. And what you need in detail on every question answered along the way, if you have any questions or get stumped on any questions throughout the whole Book. Please ensure you ask me if either provided a Q & A chapter of the platform or you can message me directly, privately, should you need to be more private.

Chapter 3

Thank you for purchasing this because their argument guides to hiring virtual assistants. Now let's get started. When it comes to running your business you have lots of tasks to complete each day. You are probably trying very hard to race ahead of your competitors and operate your business on a low global scale. But if you are thinking that you would manage it all along you are quite mistaken.

Shocked right. But it is. Oh damn it's true. Or for more than more. If we think about it you always need an extra hand of assistance for achieving great success. Moreover you can safely trust the virtual system you Kerry are many boards and asked for while you quash a tree or new next business meeting without interruption. But why delay gay tasks to a virtual assistant when you have your own assistant. Well in this chapter and in this quarter the particular I am sure you the reasons the benefits and the task that you can delegate are there to assist in or in other words v.a So to begin.

You then ask some questions that most of us ask concerning this Book or concerning this topic in particular. I consider that it is important to have them clarified before going further and we will go out and I'll answer them in the next minutes. So the questions are wondering all are there trust science reasons why you need a Virtual Assistant and does the investment on a third assistant comes back. So. Hordes of assistants. Virtual systems. Is our fallible 24/7. Him or her. It doesn't matter if there were only two hours today or if they were down to 12000. They can work until the task is complete Of course as long as they get paid. You are you as an independent.

Don't have to worry about providing an office, a telephone or a P.S. or even a deck you're off praxis. They work with their own equipment to get the job done. You just have to give that task that needs to be completed and this will resort immediately or save some money for your own company. Other attributes of a virtual assistant is that you can hire them for only how much you need them. The two main types of payments are Arly and fixed price.

The hourly payment is very economical. Companies. Like for example freelancer combines such us up for work such as freelance and a com and an employer. So they have all created apps that can be stored on the freelancer CPC. So that you as an employer can monitor all his or her walk at all times. This is it for this chapter. Thank you for reading. I should see you on the next one.

Chapter 4

In this chapter I want to talk about 16 reasons for hiring a virtual assistant. Reason number one. You cannot walk on all that asks you to have an extra hand. And it is important. I see this and it is important to have extra hands-on projects that are essential to your business. ROLF. Roomba One thing called collaboration is a powerful tool.

Trust me that would take your business to the next level. Your business can flourish with studded partnerships as short interests. So who at it won't try and expand your business bring vitale did V ace inside you process help your virtual assistant to develop a complete understanding of your business ethics and policies. Open up the virtual floor and allow him or her to share their ideas.

Eventually you will get to see substantial growth in production and it is very important because VHS can drive business growth and they can help you achieve more success. This is awful. This chapter at sea or on the next.

Chapter 5

Reason number two, access to the best talent. There are several benefits of hiring a virtual assistant. Well, your virtual assistant understands your business throughout. As a result, you would see that knowledge getting reflected in each and every task performed by them. Want to know the best part? Why hiring a VA? You don't have to be bothered about graphical restrictions.

This allows you free access to world class talent. Those better options become available at operatively lower costs. It means your business is sure to shine to communicate more with your VA. Clear would here it would be his or her ardent understanding regarding your task requirements. Gradually, the VA becomes a team member who just happens to be required to be working remotely. It's not a problem. So this is awful, this chapter. I should see you on the next one.

Chapter 6

Reason number three decreased operation costs many drippin always find it hard to cope with their expenses and it is understandable. Getting some tasks out source is one of the purrfect money saving options. Use your virtual assistant to cut down on operational expenditures by having every year you can save expenses for office space made in scores and additional access.

Moreover you don't need to purchase office equipment like computers or telephones or Internet connections to operate depending on your current need of business to support your virtuousness and walk on a part time or full time or hourly or whatever you agree on basis compared to a regular employee. A V It costs less because you do not need to pay for any employee benefits. This is it for this chapter.

Chapter 7

Reason number four reduced workload and out myself or any. Business corner. I suppose this all out. Your pass or more off than you. Important Tasks when you're overwhelmed due to the jam packed schedule. In such circumstances VHS might come in handy as they can focus on the on or several crucial tasks. They can help you for example.

Market research and data entry in or management online marketing scare call answering search engines to position web development content riding transactions and many many more. These professionals are secured in more doable areas vs candy quizzes. You walk in real distress and help you keep everything organized. They make sure that these Thar's can get completed in a simple time frame as a result. You keep running the business as smoothly as possible.

Chapter 8

REASON NUMBER FIVE focus on the core operations are really true trips you know you need more time to focus on your core business functions. Here are two things that you should take in order. Things you can do yourself and things you shouldn't be doing on your own. There would also be several tasks about which you don't have that much experience in or your ex put you know at it.

So on the other hand, looks really require direct attention. You can change it or by simply asking the detector of your routine tasks. They would provide personal as well as administrator support and provide you with more time to focus on the most crucial aspects of your business. Therefore this is why every A comes in handy and their job becomes as important as yours.

Chapter 9

Reason Number Six 24/7 availability in this present scenario just be available to cross the list for nine to 10 hours. Is it enough that having 24/7 availability helps you widen your market outreach and reach? So how can you make your business available 24/7 for customers? Well I have two assistants from a different time zone and rest assured. Why did you with your clients?

You would do the other tasks or you would be sleeping. Moreover the V.A. would be there to assist you. You even during official hold this so your business sometimes may not even take holidays, bar yourself as a business or up wood. Besides you don't have to worry about any temporary shortage of manpower with that assistant services wondering why so well it's because you will always get an extra hand and extra support a backup of another trained virtual assistant who can replace the one you work with all the time in any emergency. This is for this chapter. I should see it next.

Chapter 10

Reason number seven, pay according to the requirement now virtual assistants will bill you only for the hours they work. If you hire Vé, you don't need to think of paying for sick days, vacation days or health insurance and so on and so forth. This can save a great deal of money for you while providing you with valuable services to operate your business methodically.

You just need to pay for the time taken by your virtual assistant to do the tasks assigned or delegated by. Just know one thing in the professional var wall, no walk's means no money to be paid. This is for this chapter. I should see the next one.

Chapter 11

Reason number eight, more work and less time as an entrepreneur, you work hard to get things done while doing so, you often need to juggle with too many tasks single handedly. But why go solo when you have the option of hiring a talented Vé. Imagine using those hours to explore new business opportunities. Seems intuitively right. So well, here lies the advantage of hiring a virtual assistant.

By outsourcing tasks to your virtual assistant, you would be able to drive your business growth even further. VCs can perform tasks that are needed to be done in a regular manner, which helps you manage multiple tasks within limited time, which ultimately will lead you to having more work done and less time.

And at the same time, cheaper than you would normally pay for someone who is in your office setting while you don't have work or while you have work. So this is it for this chapter I should see on the next one.

Chapter 12

REASON NUMBER NINE improve your online presence increasing the frequency of posts in social media will strengthen the identity of your brand. Additionally you must pay heed to several aspects such as print resources to consumers. We see the creation of engaging content promotion posts and activities that can keep up with your client and your audience. However an active presence in social media requires a lot of time and persistence. Think you can manage time for that.

Probably not that much because I believe you would have more important stuff. So how can you improve your social media ? Well here are the action steps you should take. Ask your virtual assistant to offer you the best help in this field and try to find a v.a that specializes in this field.

By doing this essential thing they will help you increase their involvement with your consumer base with all sorts of relevant expertise. They can increase the frequency of bosses in social media and the identity of your brand will be strengthened significantly. This is it for this chapter.

Chapter 13

Reason Number 10 flexible walking ethics. Now virtual assistants have a flexible work schedule which means that it can be adjusted according to business needs. There are several virtual benefits of hiring a virtual assistant as they will walk for you on a project basis or on an hourly basis. So what's more, veejays can provide you with several other solutions to the business needs. So the time zone differences provide you with a greater flexibility in past management and adjustable walks schedules that can maximize the performance and increase output along with managing costs.

Therefore you would be able to hire a virtual assess in a totally different timezone while you are. Walking and doing something else. And while they are competing and they are brought in for you in a different country for example while you are operating from the United Kingdom, where I am based, you would be able to hire someone from abroad for example from Australia or from a country that has taught a different band and then you.

And while you are targeting their market you don't have to be up while they are up. Does she target them? You can do your thing and while you sleep in or whatever and have someone up in Australia Targeting your audience and are presenting your business so this is it for this chapter.

Chapter 14

Reason 11 guarantees confidentiality. One of the critical things for the optimal running of your business is building trust. And that is important. You can build a relationship of trust with your V.A.. Why in the same manner as you would do for your full time employee or employees in your office. You're V.A. ask on your behalf. He or she would work dedicatedly to protect your interests and your company's reputation.

Moreover V.A. can make you a business image more attractive to your clients. He or she would observe strategies and take preventive measures against possible market challenges that may arise in the future. Therefore that comps and that brings them an important role to have in our environment as a business. So this is a FOR THIS chapter.

Chapter 15

Reason 12 scalability in operations. What is the Turner time for delivery or deliverables in your business get slowed down. Well it indicates that you need to scale up your business. Scaling requires additional manpower so that the increase in Ward volume can be managed properly while having a virtual assistant will allow clean operations with less amount of risk. They have the efficiency to handle the additional volume of business.

The flexible nature of that just isn't allowed to manage because this is all business variables with ease while controlling expenses.

Chapter 16

Reason 13 elfish in cost the mark handily voiced support is crucial part of your business and it puts the identity and reputation of your brand on the line. However, the deadly killer of your customer service calls can be very time consuming. Bosc found a virtual assistant who can also help you in this aspect.

You can make calls to update quotes, find out information, fix appointments, connect with a business Pardoner's and gather a board and messages on your behalf or even go out of the way. Or if its They specialize in it or make a call to a Book to get you more customers. You can choose to have your V.A. manage the cause for you while you are in the midst of important work. This is a FOR THIS chapter. I should see you on it.

Chapter 17

Reason 14 week error in tripping over lack of birth control and doing the things themselves. Let's face it it's not possible to be the Jack of all trades with the trusses. We can make up for all this skill gap. Your new organization would provide you with a pipeline of x roskill sets.

If you are not tech savvy, aviators can accomplish various tasks on your behalf with the help of technology. This is one of the reasons why you need a Virtual Assistant. They will perform tasks that might seem a bit tricky to you. Therefore the war becomes more important to you. Thank you for reading this chapter. I should see next.

Chapter 18

VAs strive to provide quality service. There just isn't a committee to provide a very productive resource while delivering value to their clients. They are well aware of the fact that your business revenue also depends on the positive execution of the tasks.

The reputation of business success depends on how well they can please their clients being wholeheartedly dedicated to the work. VAs try to constantly provide high quality services at times that these assistants perform at a higher level than the confidentiality and conventionality of full time employees. Therefore, their role becomes even more important to your business success. This is what I should read in the next chapter.

Chapter 19

It's boy Important have more leisure time. Having a virtual assistant on your side allows you to have more leisure time. Identify chapters that are required. Do you direct attention and for the rest of the tasks. Assign a V8 to get those done within a time and within the time frame by offloading you Monday.

Costs are there to assess and can literally add more productive hours you day henceforth you will get some time to spend with your friends and families. Eloquent commentary market tribunals are gradually releasing the borders of delegating tasks to the V.A. in order to raise up the business. Love the mask for the rest of their limited time. This is for this chapter.

Chapter 20

In this chapter I want to talk about the investment now that we have seen the good reasons as to why you should hire a virtual assistant at the end of the day. It's the final decision that everyone has to make. So after all of the chapters and weezer's have previously talked about virtual assistants and how they're good pals, in my opinion I believe they are well walled off from their investment.

Therefore it is this time for you to make your own decision. Thank you for reading. I should see the next chapter.

Chapter 21

In this chapter I will talk about her bar tasks that you can outsource to a virtual assistant. And it is quite important to actually mention that because there are quite a few of them. Number one online research the quickest way to find information on any topic product or either or event is through online research. But conducting online research can be daunting and time consuming.

Delegate the research war to you. Virtual Assistant who would look for any kind of information on the web for you. Do not forget to share the important credentials such as IDC usernames password etc along with specific instructions to get the rest of their assistants. Number two date entry. It is one of the most repetitive ad libs who use administrative tasks that can be very well handled by their system. The work actually involves collecting data entry into spreadsheets or award documents or Google Docs weirich why sitting at a computer for a very long period of time as a virtual assistant would assume the responsibility of updating your database entries for a prolonged period of time so that he can relax and enjoy some free time.

Now the next one would be number three and that is they are. Well you are gearing up for a business meeting. Make a parliament chapter on it's one of the most essential tasks for you. But these chapters take longer hours of preparation which means a waste of your productivity being a sign these stars of day that were resonating diverge a cistern and utilize your valuable time for and Haitian you prospect of your business. All you need to do is provide clear stoushes to the V.A. and how to perform the chapter. Number four market research for age all market research is necessary to understand the industry competitiveness and its cost.

With our marketing knowledge you venture when all is held back. You can always ask your virtual assistant to conduct call market research to find relevant marketing information about your business. They'll do an extensive study on your competitors and the products I send you the findings and very organized systematic manner for easy comp.. Now Number 5 or line marketing. So Online Marketing is essential for you. If you are to expand your business or want to get more competitive advantage. But such virtual remodeling needs implementation of the office in their cliques and expertise from you which might make you think that you are just not the right person for. Poring over it.

Make your online marketing they view as a great success with the help or for a place with a wide range of online marketing tools and methods that are Sisk and do all line marketing on their clients and be. Moreover overall expertise and found knowledge in this area which would surely be left there if they found SH financial outcome of your business.

Point Number Six call answering is all business to me. Book either do your business associates or do you cost X.. Moreover, operating businesses. Business activities on an international level require you to keep your followers active all the time because a close lie might result in a loss of a good business opportunity or in a good partnership.

Share your workload and ask your virtual assistant to me or answer calls on your behalf. This would make all the necessary Books West Point to all to all and any econ Book and nor does all the board information for you in a way which you can find simple to understand. The best path you do not even need to be to the problem of the tasks Vere's would complete you does with a maze of proficiency and keep your business running even when you sleep.

Chapter 22

Number seven. Social Media Marketing in today's media age it is essential to increase brand visibility, boost sales and draw more traffic to our website. But these tasks are repetitive. Need a lot of patience. Higher secured the table can appropriately do marketing on your behalf. From generating leads to bossing the latest chapter files. These virtual assistants would never disappoint you. Rule number two is email management.

Sometimes it becomes doubting to manage YUGE volumes off in or that can we see you can we see in your inbox on a daily basis such in case a v.a comes to you. Do you race hue by yourself for example. Answer your EMA's on your behalf. Check your promotional messages and anything spam e more effectively. Number nine utterable application of all of it is quite a significant dossed in the business in our. But you can always manage the time that each business application requires.

Just find a virtual assistant who comes with specialization in application development. They can cost the Mizen you the performance of these publications with any external help, no care and any hoarded one search engine optimization. This process is more traffic to your sites from search engines through search or resource here. It is important to demote that improper s your practices can at throatily affect your business and your online status. Therefore it is always better to seek services vs books and provide effective SEO services.

They will search the relevant keywords for your articles and blog content and perform your assessments on the search engine analytics to send you a comprehensive report on the virtual status of your business. Decide that they can even write articles and blogs related to your keywords for you. Number 11 web development your website is the first thing that helps your visitors to build an image first impression that can last forever. On the Nash of your business, you offered product services. Therefore if you cannot make good sales it means that visits are not staying on your web page.

The same thing applies if you have a shop in the local area. If the front of the house is not as good as the back of your house then it is costless. Are not going to buy anything from you. Therefore opt for the professional help of VHS how can we as well as develop your website you see versus what some applications and tools such as what freres Dreamweaver jumu'ah exceptional more are they will provide you website just the right combination of graphics and content which is sure to fetch you more cost the most in the future.

No attempt to continue writing according to the rider has to understand the nature of your business and veil of content which supports your ideas and expounds on them. Therefore it is the task which requires not only expertise but all DAILY. The quad and drabby process. You can also outsource waggy tasks to be a heavy ace who can have the extra you who have the expertise in the relevant fit you skilled V.A. care right to quantify for you. Articles, websites , blogs and social media sites. After doing extensive research on the topics and delivering a resort which is up to your satisfaction this is it for this chapter. I should see you on the next one.

Chapter 23

In this view I want to give you Depp's after you hire a virtual assistant. Tip number one. Start by delegating relatively minor tasks. Even if the V.A. is a paragon of perfection on paper, don't hand off a critical assignment right away by having the V.A. handle a smile or ask first.

You can determine the best way to communicate with each other when the tasks are low. If the V.A. is going to make mistakes because he or she misunderstood your needs or because you didn't clearly describe it to them it's better to find out on less critical tasks. Or otherwise. N this is for this chapter I should see on the next one.

Chapter 24

Tip number two determines how often you will touch base with your V.A. Some clients want to schedule a weekly forkball to their V.A. while others may contract for specific projects and rarely speak with the V.A.. Regardless of the frequency and Channel or Food communication. You may want to ask you v.a what you should expect as far as the basis and what will be the best process for walking together.

What do you want? What you don't want to do is micromanage how to save you time after all. So it is very important to outline the pines and the basis with your GPA at the end of the day. They work for you so you should treat them the same way as you would treat a person who is walking for you in your office.

Therefore having a brief meeting every morning or having a brief in or every morning or having a brief call or a detailed call every week is an important aspect to actually keep up with your v.a. This is a FOR THIS chapter. I should see you on the next one.

Chapter 25

Tip number three Be as specific as possible. If you expect the V.A. to say you should. The list of venues for an event you would be hosting by Tuesday is the first thing Tuesday morning or is that the end of the day on Tuesday. Are you expecting the shortlist to consist of three venues or a dozen. Is the price more important than location?

Do you want the list to include pros and cons of each day? In all they say never assume it's best to spell out their expectations ahead of time and let the V.A. handle it from there because at the end of the day. You don't want to receive an accountant or enlist or a source. Ask for a schedule time. That is not media expectation. Therefore it is a port of despair. Coral actual men in the beginning to be specific.

For your job or the task that you want to complete rather than having them complete the hall task and wasting your time and for them your time and your money because you pay them. And not get what you are expecting to get. So it is important to outline and be as specific as possible. This is it for this chapter.

Chapter 26

Tip number of fall use cloud storage for all of your documents and use cloud services for all of your needs storing. Or will a report on the cloud ensure that they are accessible even when the Virtual Assistant v.a is not. There are many options to choose from.

For example goal would drive box and Dropbox are a few of the most popular. It is important because at the end of the day you don't want them to be walking on all of the documents and then sending you a copy that is incompatible with your system. Therefore that is important.

Actually Make sure you outline at the beginning that they should be using a specific or line Google Drive or line service that you set in place to applaud. And now Lord and even edit while down working on your projects because that way you are making sure you can access any documents and any products and any works while vig are not reachable. This is for this chapter I should see next.

Chapter 27

Tip number five Ask for suggestions after communicating on an assignment you may want to ask the V.A. if he or she had any questions, concerns or comments especially in the beginning. The V.A. may not voluntary feedback unless been asked for a similar feedback do you per your starch basis as well. Also ask if the V.A. has any suggestions regarding how to handle the task better. He or she may have developed shortcuts while walking with other clients or he or she may have the abilities and experience that you simply don't know about. Therefore it is important to ask for their suggestions and get more feedback.

This way you know that if the job you are giving them is the right job for them or it is not made for them. Therefore you need to find another virtual assistant. You don't need to be walking with someone and pay the money that at the end of the day they can be wasting your time and your money while not getting anything done. Therefore it is important to actually outline all of this and find out more information and more about your eventual access than as you would a normal employee that you would have in your office. This is it for this chapter.

Chapter 28

Hi, everyone. Well done on completing the fury part of this Book, it's time for us to jump right into the practical. And with that being said, in this chapter and in this chapter in particular, I will show you how to hire a virtual assistant. What kind of tools you should use and how you can benefit from hiring remote staff in your company.

Now, just to give you a heads up, the sort of stuff that we would be using are all mainly from Third World countries. Therefore, you would learn how to use Third World countries' help in order for you to succeed in a first world country. If you are not in a first world country or vice versa or whatever, you can just try to apply the same scenario, but with your own twist. Therefore, I will leave the judgment to you.

At the same time, what I will show you is the virtual job description that I should use, the ethics, the minimum wages, how to follow the national slavery policies, Of course, to make sure that you are who you are. He ought to be complying with the slavery rules and make sure that you're paying the correct amounts of the jobs and stuff that you're hired for. So with that being said, let's jump right into the next chapter.

Chapter 29

So without having to go through the on Polumbo, we're going to go straight into the juicy stuff. So now we're going to talk about the advantages and disadvantages of hiring a freelancer from abroad. So the advantage, as you can see from the screen, is that there are five key advantages that I think are top that anyone could, should look into when hiring a staff from abroad.

Number one is the low costs. Then you have the more time for you, the economic rates, the time differences, as well as the area of work, which gives you an advantage over your competitors as you would have someone doing something. It only specifically and that would give you results the same as you would have someone doing it from the local office at your local residents.

Now, no. The next step would be to talk about the disadvantages. So the disadvantages which we have experienced in our companies are four things. Number one is communication. You would have a lot of communication problems, especially if you are in an area where there are electricity problems or there are Internet issues or any of that sort. Therefore, make sure when you do your interview, you ask your staff about the electricity. Do they have any downtime?

When was the last time that they had a downtime telephone or Internet service? Is there any issues around you, questions such as how many megabytes per second? You get all of those. And that would give you an idea of if the person that you're hiring is in a good area or an area that you can basically work from or not, because effectively that would hurt you in the long run. The next one would be the differences. So if you were to hire someone locally, then you have the cultural religion, the same, et cetera.

However, if you were to hire someone from abroad, then you don't know those. And that could create a conflict or create a confusion and a misunderstanding between each other. Therefore, that is a difference which you need to clarify from the get go. Another one is there is no personal supervision, so it is not as if you would open the door and walk into the office and see the staff working right there. And then it essentially is online that working from their own home. So there is no personal supervision, which is a disadvantage to you.

And finally, you have the data security. So data security us, as we all know, gdb all privacy policies, all of those are very, very important and essential for any successful business. Therefore, you need to put policies in place that would allow you to basically have somewhat control over the access that you give to your staff. And then at the same time, it will allow you to control the data that they see from your own companies.

So we will talk about Daschle, loss, loss, all of those tools that would allow you to give access. But without further ado, let's jump right onto the salaries and why the country I've chosen is cheap and why you should choose it. So read out for them in the chapter.

Chapter 30

Perfect. So with that being said, let's jump right into why the low cost to you. So I'm currently up on the government's website for the Philippine government's National Wages and Productivity Commission. Therefore, I just want to point out that the daily minimum wage rates for the Philippines are those. So if we were to, for example, take the most expensive than the highest paid, which is in the region of NCR, that is basically the capital region. I will go ahead and put this here.

Filipino pestis, two dollars, and that would be ten years dollars per day. So if you were to hire someone from the capital of the Philippines, you would hire them essentially at 10 U.S. dollars per day. If you were to hire them for the full one month, then you would be looking at about 30 days Pym's, and that is essentially 300 U.S. dollars per day. So. You might ask yourself, why would you basically target that? So what I want to point out is how you should structure your payments. So the payment that you would pay to your staff would essentially have to be the national salary plus the experience and the skills. So you'd basically have to judge yourself by the job that you are giving them.

Is it good for the salary as well as the experience? And therefore, if you're hiring someone more advanced, then your solution essentially goes up. If you're an entry person or a trainee or anything other than the salary would essentially be close to the national minimum wage. With that being said, you might ask yourself, why would you basically find someone to hire from the

Philippines? So the number one you have gone through and seen the advantages and disadvantages that I've mentioned.

But basically another one that you essentially can say is a top priority is the language in the Philippines, they in the school and universities, etc.. Educators tend to teach their students American English. Therefore, your employee or your staff or your freelancer would have a good knowledge of English. And that is the help. And using the help of platforms and tools such as grumbly, etc., you might have basically hit the jackpot. So you might want to, let's say, double check, double talk and see what your employer would do and what not.

But essentially, that would give you the upper hand in that case. Now, speaking of the payments, you can basically literally type on Google the minimum wage of the country, and that is the year and the per day. So that would give you essentially the minimum salary for daily rates of the country that you're targeting.

In my opinion, the Philippines is one of the top countries that you should focus on. But you can go for the likes of Thailand. You can go for the likes of India, Pakistani, et cetera. But from our experience, I think the Philippines starts at the top. So with that being said, let's jump right to the chapter of where you can find the staff and how you should go about it.

Chapter 31

Now that we have talked about the salary and how much you should be paying, you're a remote staff. It's time for us to look at the platforms you should use in order to hire these staff. So we have Upwork, which is almost the first chosen platform when it comes to online freelance hiring. But the next platform for our case would be online Filipino jobs. So online jobs, the Philippine would be the platform that you should look at as well.

Our doctor I'll talk about Upwork first and then take you through the online jobs in the Philippines later on. So I have been a user of Upwork for quite some time now. And when I joined, I signed up for a freelance account as well, because I wanted to check what other business people are posting on there, how much they're paying their staff, and basically compare questions, interview questions, answers, job descriptions and all of that stuff from the platform. So therefore, I am able to post something that is relevant and would be actually good for the remote staff. So with that being said, what would happen is if you're too if you have a freelance account now, I do want to mention that Apple does limit the amount of times that you are able to sign up as a freelancer. And a lot of the time they ask you to verify.

And the majority of the time that I have heard of it is that there are declining users in competitive areas. Therefore, they want to limit the amount of freelancers they have applying for jobs, et cetera. But if you're a freelancer, what you should do is use it to your advantage. And that is by searching for the job that you're trying to create in order for you to find the stuff before. So I quickly typed virtual assistant, and I was able to find multiple job posts. In fact, there are over 10000 job posts found all around the world. And those range between skills, services, tools, etc. So you can see here the salary that they are paying is five to 10 years per hour.

Now, I do want to mention that Upwork limits you to three U.S. dollars minimum per hour. Therefore, that could be a problem for you when starting out, because you might not be able to pay the three year dollars per hour for staff. You might be surprised how many people are not able to afford this, especially when you are starting out. But with online jobs, Phillipine, it allows you to do that. And I will explain to you in a minute how you are able to see here hourly rate, three to 10 U.S. dollars intermediate, and you're able to read about it and open it and see what you can take from it as an inspiration and apply it to your own. This right here is a job loss that we have posted ourselves. We have used workable.

Workable is one of the top platforms that we use ourselves in order to find job descriptions. They have over 700 job descriptions. I would highly recommend them for you to use. What you would do is essentially visit resources, not workable, as you can see here, and you scroll down if you want, you can filter it by category or you can best go through here. In our case, we can go and type a virtual assistant. And you are able to see this. Now, I've opened it on a new tab already. So this is the job brief that they have. This is their responsibilities and this is the requirements. So you are able to copy them, create a new job on Upwork and paste that in there.

Now, moving on from Upwork, let's move on to online jobs, the Philippines, online jobs of Philippines. I'm going to go to their homepage because essentially that is where you will land when you visit them. So you will basically come to online jobs, the Philippines, and you'll scroll down and click on view more Filipino resinous us. You would basically be taken to this page. You are able to select and choose what kind of job you are basically looking to hire for. So you just put it here. So in our case, if we have virtual assistants, we will click that and we will be taken to a new tab, which essentially is this tab right here, but sometimes takes a lot of time, a long time to load.

So I'll close it for now. But you will be taken to this page right here to list down all of the jobseekers in that particular field that you are looking to hire for. So right here, you are able to see that this person is an I.T. specialist and a client and care specialist, sort of I.T. specialist slash client care specialist. And you are able to see some brief information about them. So the availability of work is over 30 hours per week. So they are able to work for you over 30 hours a week. And their education is bachelor's degree, which is quite good for the type of job that you would basically hire, essentially, especially sorry, especially if it's virtual assistants. Here you are able to see the expected salary, and that is 15000 per month.

Now, the one thing that you should be aware of and always make for your checking is the ID proof idea proof is a school that online jobs Philippine gives to this particular worker. This particular job seeker based on the idea that they have provided on their face. So it will be taken through facial recognition, either automatic or manual. And then they will be scored based on that. And you will see how legitimate it is from the submission that's submitted. So that is 70. Here you have 99. Here you have 80. I personally like to stick to 80 plus. So anybody above 80, that is perfect because I can later on.

Awesome to open a camera or do a chapter camera interview and essentially see if they are genuine or not. Because you do not want to fall into the trap of being in a scamps hands and essentially hire somebody who is not who they say they are. So you are able to see the top skills, et cetera, et cetera. So here you are able to see the expected salary that they are looking for, for the monthly. And that is based on, I believe, 30 hours per week. So they are looking for 15000 pesos. So that would be 306. If we were to hire 30.

The hours on Upwork, if we were to hire 30 hours per week by four, that is 120, 120 by three years, you would be looking at 360 to pay up. And that is without having to pay the processing fees. So if you're to pay 360 to Upwork, you would ultimately look at paying 306 users directly to this staff on online jobs. But please bear in mind that for all online jobs, BHB essentially is a paid platform and you would have to pay in order for you to use it. It is not too bad because you are able to use it for free. So if you are to go for basically more features, then you are able to jump on to the 69 per month at the plan or the premium plan, depending on what you are looking for.

So with that being said, I usually like to search the cost of living in the Philippines and see whether the cost of living, as well as the cost of the task of the employee is matching with the national kind of cost of living. So I usually like to do is I usually type on

Google cost of living in the Philippines to make sure that I am safe and my staff are safe because I do not want to hire someone and make them work as a slave and basically take them through that hassle without me even realizing what I'm getting them into and being a part of a problem that I am not even realizing on be part of. So it is basically very, very important to know that. So you are able to select the city that you basically want to look for.

But essentially, I would want to leave it blank for the sake of this chapter. But as you can see here, a family of four estimated monthly costs are about one thousand seven hundred U.S. dollars. So that is a family of four by four to look at a single person. Then they are essentially looking at about 26000 without rent. Now, here, cost of living is on average 45 percent lower than the United States. If you go down here, you are able to see the inexpensive restaurants or if you're if that person wants to eat at an inexpensive restaurant, then they would, let's say, pay 150 pesos. If they were to eat at a three Book meal, a mid-range restaurant, that would be paying about 1000 pests, and that would be a meal for two.

And then if you scroll down here, kind of the important bits, eggs, that would be about eight or nine loaf of fresh bread, that would be 53 water. That would be about 38. And kind of transportation, Tenu, 10 pesos for a one way ticket, local transport. And if they wanted to have a regular kind of post, then I would be paying Varvaris 57. And I believe that is on a monthly and for rent per month if you are to rent a one bedroom apartment in the city center. That is about 16000 outside of the city center. That is eight thousand seven hundred. So essentially you would be looking around the cities. But you need to also be aware that a lot of the people living in the Philippines own properties. So that is what it is their own, whether it is family or parents. It is very, very important to ask and see whether they own the property or not.

I know it might be a personal question, but that would give you an idea of whether on the long run that person would, let's say, disappear out of the the the the basically the whole scene and out of the whole picture, or there would be a good long term, because if they are going to be struggling financially, then there would not be an issue. So there would be an issue for you in the long run. So it is very important to ask these kinds of questions, which are our basic points, our next article for you to see what kind of question you should ask, and then I will describe why you should actually ask these questions. So with that being said, look out of the next chapter where I would be showing you what kind of questions you ask.

Chapter 32

As we have discussed, the platforms that you would have to use in order to find the freelancer's. Now I want to find them. I want to talk to you about the kind of questions you want to ask if we want to make sure you're all on the same page. I have noticed a lot of mistakes when an employer or a business person posts a job on Upwork, on online jobs, in the Philippines or any of the platforms.

One thing that they find is, oh, what you would like to do in your free time, what you would like to do. Let's talk about your day to day and all that stuff. Now, essentially, those questions are good to build relationships with your employees, build team skills, all of that. But when you're doing a hiring, when you're in the hiring stage, it is very important to find how you can best manage and best improve the service of your company, as well as to get basically the most out of the skills your team members have.

So, frankly, knowing what they like to do day to day or the kind of hobby like drawing that I would like to do, it won't help you in the long run in the company. It might help you, for example, if you have a job that you would like, for example, to do some painting or some graphic design, then that would essentially help you knowing what kind of hobby they have and all that stuff. But essentially, if you are an ecommerce or online business, the type of questions you need to ask is what's on the screen essentially easy to find?

What are the areas of expertise they have? Therefore, it gives you an advantage over your competitors. And you can assign them to that particular job and that particular task instead of you mind finding someone who does everything. Because, frankly, if I go to the hospital and I, for example, have a heart issue or heart problem, would I really go and choose a doctor that knows everything about the body and basically like a general practitioner? Or would I go and choose the heart doctor who specializes in heart and all of that? So I would ultimately choose the heart, the heart of it, because that is the speciality of that doctor. Therefore, it is very important for you to find the kind of expertise and experience that this employee has.

Another thing is you ask them, how long have you been in, let's say, a virtual assistant role for. So they'll tell you, I've been here two years, three years, three months, because if someone is in you, then ultimately you want to stay away from them temporarily. Or if you wanted to take the chance, I would more than encourage you to give them the chance and see how the waters are. Other than that, you need to ask them questions such as which tools do you like to use? So what kind of tools do they like to use when it comes to business?

So what is that day to day tools that they use, etc. because that gives you an advantage over previous competitors that they might have worked with. You might not be a direct competitor with a company that they work for or have worked for. However, if they have worked for a marketing agency and you are hiring someone who specializes in marketing and there are freelancers and all of those, before you hire them, another marketing agency has hired them. What you want to use is the experience and skills that they have had from the previous employer to your advantage. So you would ask them what kind of tools you used?

And you would start asking these questions as soon as you know that they have worked for another agency or another business similar to yours, because that way it will allow you as a business to improve on the tools you have. So if you have a tool that is outdated and another agency is using a newer one, then that will give you the upper hand to you actually updating your systems and start using modern tools, the latest updates. So literally you got it for free. Ultimately, just from having a job interview. So the other one is, what else do you like to work?

Because you are in, let's say, the UK or the United States and you have someone from the Philippines, you have eight hours difference. So when it's nine a.m. here in the UK, it's four p.m. in what we call in the Philippines, I believe it's seven hours different. Sorry. And therefore, it is very important to find out whether that freelancer is willing to work from four to, let's say, midnight for your company. So it is very, very important. Some of them like to work early in the day. Some of them, if you have a job such as email marketing specialist, then they can work their job at any time because it's just them scheduling emails. So that would go out in our time zone or your local time zone.

The next question would be, how do you prefer to communicate? So as a company yourself, you should have a standard operating procedure on the count of. Communication channel that you should have for the whole internal team. But you should. You might as well ask your staff or the new intern. Then you come up on what kind of channels they are used to, because if they are used to the channels that you have within the company, then that will save you on training. And then you have the next question: what city of, let's say, the Philippines do you live in? Because that gives you more room to research on the city, because if you know the city and you are able to search online, then you will find out whether it has bad things or good things or electricity problems or Internet speed, et cetera.

The next question would be, what is your Internet speed, because your main job is to literally operate via the Internet. So that is very, very important for you to find out why it is important for you and them to use the Internet. So. So you tell them what you're going to speed. So they will tell you, for example, my dad's voice, let's say 20 megabytes per second, or if you are in the UK, you most likely have a half a gigabyte by three, depending on the area they live in, etc. So if they're living in an area, they have only one gigabyte, one megabyte per second, and you will have difficulty communicating with them, talking to them. Then that would be an issue for you in the long run. So if you want to save the headache, you should look into asking these questions.

The next question is you want to find out if they have ever had any downtime with their Internet, because if they have, then you need to find out. Is it a regular? Is it not regular? Does it happen often? Not often. All of that, because that, again, would help you to make the right and informative decision on whether you should hire that person or not. The next question would be the electricity, because electricity would be the next after Internet speed and Internet in general, although electricity powers the Internet by Internet speeds since not many.

A lot of the countries, a lot of the developed countries, such as the Philippines, do have electricity, but every now and then they do have power cuts. So it's very important for you to find out if there is any downside of electricity in their area and if they have ever had any power cuts. So that would be on the next question. Now, the final question that I like to ask from my own personal experience is, do they have a family of their own, as in me having a child, direct child or not asking my father or my mother or anything like that? No, no. As in me being married or me having a child on my own, or am I single or do I basically have a family or are they single?

You might ask. Oh, that's a strange question. Or why would someone ask that question? Not from my experience. I have found out that married people, it might sound crazy, but it's actually very true. Married people or a parent is more likely to be lower than you and more close and be more productive in your company than a single person. It might be biased and I might be basically once hiding. But from my experience and from the hires that I have done from the Philippines, that is essentially the case.

I have found both parties singles, and I've hired basically both singles and parents. And I've always found that parents are always the ones that stick around the longest. And I'll tell you why, because parents have responsibility at the end of the day. So if somebody has a responsibility to me every single day, and that is basically to to work hard, to earn money for their family, earn money basically for to to live on and and basically basic living expenses. And there is family involved and all that stuff. Then that would give them more need and more pay. They would want to stick around your company even more.

And that would bring me to the next point, which I would like to mention at some point in this chapter. And that would be the Karpis. So that would be basically the commission that you should be giving this stuff. So from our expert, from my experience and the whole team in my home, the whole team experience is hiring someone who is at merit is a lot better than hiring a single person, because a single person could tell you, I can work from anywhere. I would work from here, I would work from there.

Please don't take this on board as if I'm telling you, go hire only a married person. Just give me the heads up from my own experience, how I have found it. So, yeah, so someone who is married with kids and children is responsible to take care of that. We don't want to lose their job. And it would take them a lot longer to find a different job if there was to basically leave the company at any point. So those are the 12 golden questions that I would like to quote from our interviews, because we need to find the important juicy questions that would give us a resource, not only for now, but on the long run of the company. So that being said, please read out for the next chapter.

Important Interview Questions

List What Are Your Areas of Expertise?

How Long Have You Been a <JOB ROLE> for?

Which Tools Do You Like Using?

What Hours Do You Work?

What Is Your Availability?

How Do You Prefer to Communicate?

What city of <X> do you live in?

What is your internet speed?

Do you ever get any internet downtime?

How is the electricity in your area?

When was the last time you had a power cut?

Do you have a family of your own or are you single?

Chapter 34

Now that we have spoken about the platforms, it's time for us to post our first job on Upwork. So without further ado, let's jump right on to Upwork and let's suppose the job. So you have logged into your Upwork account, you'll click on a post and you will be taken to the next page, and that is for you to select the kind of post you would like to do. So we can always use our previous job posts that we have created to save us time. Or if not, then what we can do is create a brand new one from scratch. But for the sake of this chapter, what I want to do is I want to essentially reuse one of my previous templates and change it a tiny bit in order for us to play around. So I will basically use the virtual assistant here and here.

What I'm going to do is I'm going to change the five to two. We are looking for an email marketing associate. Bear in mind that we are actually looking for an immunogen associate. Therefore, if you are looking for a higher salary, please send an email to H.R. at Ionis dot com. So I will do is I'll choose the Jocketty, you know that this email marketing skills, the skills would be ultimately email, email, marketing, content, writing, lead generation copywriting, marketing strategy, automation, campaign monitoring and emotionally that normal chimp, because we have different tools that we use marketing services to digital to tracking analytics. Yes. Yes. Lead nurturing. Yes. Active, contained.

None of these tools. Industry, B2B, we are mainly B2B. Therefore, that is the experience that we are looking for, business experience. We will keep up to whatever has been chosen. So let me see this. So next on the scope of your work, that is medium. Yes. We don't want to basically scare them away and say it's complex or that, because essentially it is not complex with the right training. Everything is medium and everything is easy. So the job would be ultimately for more than six months. Absolutely correct. And we are looking for non non nonexperts, Of course, no entry. So we were going to go in the middle and walk the region that we are going to be targeting is actually the Philippines. And we can put other countries on board for this for the sake of this job. We are particularly looking for the Philippines, but it's down to you how you want to basically select it. Therefore, for us, we are going to go with

Philippines and now we're going to choose the budget. So our budget would be between. So he tells you the professionals tend to charge between 11 to 30 years. Now, bear in mind that I am a marketing associate, and don't necessarily have to work full time. They can work one hour, two hours a day for every single day of the week. Or they can work two, three days of the week for a full on eight hour shift. So that is, again, another agreement that you would have to have with your sales staff. So here would be from three years ago. That's easy. If I put in one year's dollars, it will. Oh, actually, it allows for if I put one to one. That would be an issue, because the minimum hourly rate on Upwork is three years.

So I would put three, three years dollars to eight US cents. And here you can see the professionals and how much they're charging. But that would ultimately be from four freelancers based in first world countries such as the United Kingdom, the

United States, etc. So they don't give you this information here, but it is a bit of a sneaky way of trying to allow you to basically increase the hourly rate, but stick to what we discussed before. And that is based on the notion of national living wage or national minimum wage, as well as their skills. So how can I put in 10 years and then somebody with two years that has skills come to me and apply for the job? But because the interview didn't happen, I was wasting my time.

And ultimately, they would be wasting their time, but they will win if I go ahead and say, OK, let's hire them. But what I will do is I will give it to our interview people within that range, because I would know that the people who have applied for the job are based on the people that are looking for the skills and that they have the skills and experience that I'm looking for. So now I'll go ahead and review your post. And it will allow us to ultimately post it so you can see we're looking. Absolutely. And now for the description, what I will do is I would go ahead and change it to the template for mockable. So we're going to basically copy this. And we're going to stay in here and we are going to quickly.

Actually, that's not a good way, but what I will do is I will ultimately put it over and I will get back to you in a minute. Perfect. And just like that, we have got our job post. So with that being said, I basically tweaked it to our own needs and we said we are looking for our talents in email marketing associate to take the lead with our email marketing strategy and campaigns. And therefore, I have listed the responsibilities. I have listed the requirements, as well as the tools that will be used and the product offers and benefits. So they know what they basically are getting themselves into in terms of the commissions and KPIs.

I'll show you how you should structure them in the next chapter. And that would basically allow you to see what kind of motivates the staff to keep going and keep working hard in order to generate more sales and more leads, especially if you're hiring sales associates and sales representatives for the company. So that being said, we have gone ahead and created the campaign. Now, we know that it is a medium more than six months and all the levels that we're looking for. And then we'll go ahead and post the job after we post the job. OK, but we've done so. Congratulations on your job. Post is now live once we are on this screen.

We all have to start inviting freelancers over to the platform. So over to the job post. So we have 15 invites left. So what I would like to do is filter down now. And I want to put the job success rate at 90 percent plus because we do not want to work with anyone, 80 percent and below or 90 percent below in our case. And what we want to do, since our hourly rate is between three to eight, we would put tenuous dollars and below four hours build. I'd like to put 100 plus because they don't want to work with anyone who has worked minimum hours. So 100 plus hours would be good. If you essentially go four thousand plus, it would essentially be experts. So we don't want to go there just yet. So we will go 100 plus below 1000.

And the earned amount who don't want to basically hire somebody who is completely new. So we want to show that they have earned at least 1000 U.S. dollars in terms of the locations. What we want to do is we want to target the country that we want to target. And that is my beloved Philippines. So here in the Philippines and therefore all of the candidates that would pop up are going to be essentially from the Philippines. One final thing that I like to do when I basically go through Upwork is I like to hire freelancers and not agencies. So make sure that the talent type is always freelancers and not agencies, because essentially agencies are just an extra added to your hourly rate.

I hope that these agencies will take us without even an idea for us. So if you are hiring somebody for a printer that cost 50000, 60000, or a big project with big money in it, that essentially you would have to hire an agency because you need to make sure your money is protected, first of all, and that you are working with professionals in that sense. So in our cases, we are going to be managing them directly. And I want to be accessing kind of very, very sensitive or highly sensitive information. It is basically normal for us to go with freelancers. Hey, we are able to basically see the freelancers. So we have got a few. I'm just going to close this very quickly. We have got 15 invites left. So those are the three invites. So I will go ahead and do it if this person is admin work data. So it's not really good.

We are looking for somebody who knows marketing. So this person right here has got some marketing skills. We can invite them and interview them and see what kind of skills and what kind of help they can give us of that eight years lead generation and Web research. That could be a good idea. Let me go down here. Let's see. So we're essentially going to keep going until we find good staff to hire. So with that being said, what I will do is I will go through all of the list and I will show you afterwards the staff that I've hired and why I have hired them. So please wait on. So we have sent the last job now, so I'll go ahead and click on the invited freelancers.

I'll quickly show you the freelancers we have invited. So as you can see, all of them have a 100 percent job success rate. So therefore, if they are not all of us, a majority of them. So if we are going to hire this person right here, for example, we are guaranteeing that they have earned over 30000 U.S. dollars with 100 percent job success rate. It's kind of tricky when it comes to hiring these freelancers, because you need to make sure they are kind of meeting deadlines that are following through. They are doing what they are expected to do.

And that success rate just shows you partially if they are committed to their job and they are going to execute the job successfully. So, yeah. So as you can see, this person has got 96 percent. And I have got email marketing, essentially. That's pretty much it for the freelancers. So right now, we are going to wait for them to get back to us and then we will start the whole process. So that being said, let's jump right into the next chapter.

Chapter 35

Now that we are coming to the end of our practical chapter, I just want to jump in and show you ourselves. The staff incentive plan, which is essentially a plan that every single company that does digital work should have in place in order to give their staff goals to meet. And, Of course, targets to reach, etc.. So with that being said, I'm going to quickly show you the incentive that we have in our companies.

Bear in mind that this is an actual real plan that we use. However, data has been changed for the sake of this chapter. Therefore, without further ado, let's jump into it. So each staff member will basically be eligible for a percentage of self. So, for example, if they sell something at 1000 pounds and our agreement is to give them 10 percent commission from that, then they will get 10 percent commission. However, that 10 percent commission would be split into three into a ratio of three. And the ratio would be 60, 30 and 10, 60 percent of that 10 percent would be paid one immediately or on their pay scale.

The 30 percent would only be paid if they meet the KPI for that month. And then the 10 percent will be paid only once they reach a certain period of time within the company. That always is a good idea for them to keep them going and for them to basically try and meet more goals. So with that being said, the commission categories are here. So there is always silver, gold and platinum. And with that being said, this is the pricing for each category. That this is the commission type that we have. So the commission type we have is commission percentage, AZO

US Commission per case. So the commission percentage would be 10 percent. And then the commission per case would be the standard, let's say, rate of an agreed to pounds or two or three pounds or whatever currency you are dealing with.

Now, there are some remarks on these deals, and those are literally here. If you want, you can pause the chapter and have a look at them. But essentially, the main problem is if the deal is canceled, then they don't get a payment. If the staff resigns and there is 50 percent deducted deduction in the incentive plan they have if it sells stuff. Basically, it's not meeting KPIs, then Of course, they're not going to be paid for them, et cetera. Now, in terms of the KPIs, we are basically working here. Those are the weights that we get off the scores that we need to keep for each kind of role that we need to keep in or each type of task or feedback or speciality, if you want to say it that way. So what we focus on is the lead generation process and the quality assurance, because we need to always make sure our company is reaching high standards, as well as meeting customer expectations and always achieving high and five star reviews.

So the next option and the final one would be the new customer order. So that would be for the marketing specialist, because the market especially will basically get the leads and all that. And then they would pass it on to the social preventative who is going to try and close the deal. So that 's basically just as cost is the market, especially the weightage. However, for the sales team, it would be all the replacement team how they want to call it. It would be based on these five. So the core completion rate would have to be 90 percent plus. Strike rates would have to be seventy five percent plus quality assurance, 80 percent plus on the delivery of invoices for total value. All of that would have to be over 95 percent. And then the customer satisfaction rate would have to be over 95 percent.

As you can see, it's high standards. Therefore, if they do want to earn their commission, it is very, very important for them to actually focus on their work. So as you can see here, this is essentially what Mr. William did, for example, marketing specialists. They have a total of 23 U.S. dollars. That would be getting paid, 14 of them, because they have 60 percent commission of that. And then that would be getting paid 30 percent commission because they have met the KPIs. And then, too, they would be getting after a while because they have met the or actually essentially because they have already met the 10 percent incentive. So that that percent of their stay in the company or the period that they have been with is within the company here.

The total that they are eligible for is, Of course. So the total amount that I qualified for is 23. However, the total eligible amount that they are eligible for is 20. So those here together are 20, so 23 minus 20. It's sort of 23, yes, 20, 30, minus 20 is three. Therefore, there will not be getting paid for three different cases. On the other hand, Miss Rose is a social preventative and she has closed the doors of 925, which should be getting paid 60 percent of that. So that is the 555. And then she would be qualified for a hundred and sixty eight U.S. dollars because she has met the 30 percent KPI for that particular month.

And then here, that would be a 10 percent off because she has bypassed her time stay in the company or the probation period or whatever. She would be only 23 percent. Therefore, out of the qualified 925, she's eligible for only eight hundred and sixteen. The difference is 110. So that is essentially what she's losing, because she did not meet either the KPI or the basic time of the company. So that essentially checks that we have in place. And as you can see here, you can basically notice on the next one the best kind of numbers that they have sought every single time they are eligible for something.

They will see it here. So if they have made the grant or two of nine, nine thousand or 300, they will be basically earning this amount. So essentially, that's pretty much for the incentives and commissions. If you have any questions, please feel free to message me directly or post them in the Q&A chapter. I will get back to you shortly. Other than that, I look forward to seeing you in the next conclusion chapter. Thank you.

Chapter 36

As we have approached the end of this Book I want to end it with a definition that I love by Michael Brody and the definition of a virtual assistant is low cost life saver.

That gives you your life back and that is very very important because it is his virtual assistant intimately that will actually give you life back why not have you in having them in the office. This is a FOR THIS chapter. I hope to see you on Next. Thank you.

Conclusion

I just want to take this moment to say thank you so much for purchasing this Book. And thank you for reading the guide to how to be a virtual assistant with myself and keep us healthy. You're more comfortable under Sandy verge of sex than and how important they are for you and your business.

If you are interested in learning more please check out my other Books I teach by going to my profile where new Books are added or that I look forward to the next chapter when I give you a coupon code to use. Or my Books to get them at a discounted rate. And a little bonus: my email and my website are on this screen. You can email me at any time. I am more than happy to get back to you.

You can check out my website for more information on Barney and I have my social media. If you want to connect with me. Thank you once again and hope to see you in one of my other Books.

www.ingramcontent.com/pod-product-compliance
Lightning Source LLC
Chambersburg PA
CBHW070124230526
45472CB00004B/1409